LESSON

PLANNER

NAME: _____

PHONE: _____

LESSON *Planner*

SUBJECT / COURSE:

TOPIC: DATE:

GOAL: LESSON DURATION:

LESSON OBJECTIVES

SUMMARY OF TASKS / ACTION PLAN

MATERIALS / EQUIPMENT

REFERENCES

HOME WORK / TASKS

FEEDBACK

LESSON *Planner*

SUBJECT / COURSE:

TOPIC:

GOAL:

DATE:

LESSON DURATION:

LESSON OBJECTIVES

SUMMARY OF TASKS / ACTION PLAN

MATERIALS / EQUIPMENT

REFERENCES

HOME WORK / TASKS

FEEDBACK

LESSON *Planner*

SUBJECT / COURSE:

TOPIC: DATE:

GOAL: LESSON DURATION:

LESSON OBJECTIVES

SUMMARY OF TASKS / ACTION PLAN

MATERIALS / EQUIPMENT	REFERENCES

HOME WORK / TASKS	FEEDBACK

LESSON *Planner*

SUBJECT / COURSE:

TOPIC: DATE:

GOAL: LESSON DURATION:

LESSON OBJECTIVES

SUMMARY OF TASKS / ACTION PLAN

MATERIALS / EQUIPMENT	REFERENCES

HOME WORK / TASKS	FEEDBACK

LESSON *Planner*

SUBJECT / COURSE:

TOPIC: DATE:

GOAL: LESSON DURATION:

LESSON OBJECTIVES

SUMMARY OF TASKS / ACTION PLAN

MATERIALS / EQUIPMENT

REFERENCES

HOME WORK / TASKS

FEEDBACK

LESSON *Planner*

SUBJECT / COURSE:

TOPIC: DATE:

GOAL: LESSON DURATION:

LESSON OBJECTIVES

SUMMARY OF TASKS / ACTION PLAN

MATERIALS / EQUIPMENT

REFERENCES

HOME WORK / TASKS

FEEDBACK

LESSON *Planner*

SUBJECT / COURSE:

TOPIC: DATE:

GOAL: LESSON DURATION:

LESSON OBJECTIVES

SUMMARY OF TASKS / ACTION PLAN

MATERIALS / EQUIPMENT

REFERENCES

HOME WORK / TASKS

FEEDBACK

LESSON *Planner*

SUBJECT / COURSE:

TOPIC:

GOAL:

DATE:

LESSON DURATION:

LESSON OBJECTIVES

SUMMARY OF TASKS / ACTION PLAN

MATERIALS / EQUIPMENT	REFERENCES

HOME WORK / TASKS	FEEDBACK

LESSON *Planner*

SUBJECT / COURSE:

TOPIC: DATE:

GOAL: LESSON DURATION:

LESSON OBJECTIVES

SUMMARY OF TASKS / ACTION PLAN

MATERIALS / EQUIPMENT	REFERENCES

HOME WORK / TASKS	FEEDBACK

LESSON *Planner*

SUBJECT / COURSE:

TOPIC:

GOAL:

DATE:

LESSON DURATION:

LESSON OBJECTIVES

SUMMARY OF TASKS / ACTION PLAN

MATERIALS / EQUIPMENT

REFERENCES

HOME WORK / TASKS

FEEDBACK

LESSON *Planner*

SUBJECT / COURSE:

TOPIC: DATE:

GOAL: LESSON DURATION:

LESSON OBJECTIVES

SUMMARY OF TASKS / ACTION PLAN

MATERIALS / EQUIPMENT

REFERENCES

HOME WORK / TASKS

FEEDBACK

LESSON *Planner*

SUBJECT / COURSE:

TOPIC:

GOAL:

DATE:

LESSON DURATION:

LESSON OBJECTIVES

SUMMARY OF TASKS / ACTION PLAN

MATERIALS / EQUIPMENT

REFERENCES

HOME WORK / TASKS

FEEDBACK

LESSON *Planner*

SUBJECT / COURSE:

TOPIC:

GOAL:

DATE:

LESSON DURATION:

LESSON OBJECTIVES

SUMMARY OF TASKS / ACTION PLAN

MATERIALS / EQUIPMENT	REFERENCES

HOME WORK / TASKS	FEEDBACK

LESSON *Planner*

SUBJECT / COURSE:

TOPIC: DATE:

GOAL: LESSON DURATION:

LESSON OBJECTIVES

SUMMARY OF TASKS / ACTION PLAN

MATERIALS / EQUIPMENT	REFERENCES

HOME WORK / TASKS	FEEDBACK

LESSON *Planner*

SUBJECT / COURSE:

TOPIC: DATE:

GOAL: LESSON DURATION:

LESSON OBJECTIVES

SUMMARY OF TASKS / ACTION PLAN

MATERIALS / EQUIPMENT

REFERENCES

HOME WORK / TASKS

FEEDBACK

LESSON *Planner*

SUBJECT / COURSE:

TOPIC: DATE:

GOAL: LESSON DURATION:

LESSON OBJECTIVES

SUMMARY OF TASKS / ACTION PLAN

MATERIALS / EQUIPMENT

REFERENCES

HOME WORK / TASKS

FEEDBACK

LESSON *Planner*

SUBJECT / COURSE:

TOPIC: **DATE:**

GOAL: **LESSON DURATION:**

LESSON OBJECTIVES

SUMMARY OF TASKS / ACTION PLAN

MATERIALS / EQUIPMENT	REFERENCES

HOME WORK / TASKS	FEEDBACK

LESSON *Planner*

SUBJECT / COURSE:

TOPIC: DATE:

GOAL: LESSON DURATION:

LESSON OBJECTIVES

SUMMARY OF TASKS / ACTION PLAN

MATERIALS / EQUIPMENT	REFERENCES

HOME WORK / TASKS	FEEDBACK

LESSON *Planner*

SUBJECT / COURSE:

TOPIC: DATE:

GOAL: LESSON DURATION:

LESSON OBJECTIVES

SUMMARY OF TASKS / ACTION PLAN

MATERIALS / EQUIPMENT

REFERENCES

HOME WORK / TASKS

FEEDBACK

LESSON *Planner*

SUBJECT / COURSE:

TOPIC: DATE:

GOAL: LESSON DURATION:

LESSON OBJECTIVES

SUMMARY OF TASKS / ACTION PLAN

MATERIALS / EQUIPMENT	REFERENCES

HOME WORK / TASKS	FEEDBACK

LESSON *Planner*

SUBJECT / COURSE:

TOPIC: DATE:

GOAL: LESSON DURATION:

LESSON OBJECTIVES

SUMMARY OF TASKS / ACTION PLAN

MATERIALS / EQUIPMENT	REFERENCES

HOME WORK / TASKS	FEEDBACK

LESSON *Planner*

SUBJECT / COURSE:

TOPIC:

DATE:

GOAL:

LESSON DURATION:

LESSON OBJECTIVES

SUMMARY OF TASKS / ACTION PLAN

MATERIALS / EQUIPMENT	REFERENCES

HOME WORK / TASKS	FEEDBACK

LESSON *Planner*

SUBJECT / COURSE:

TOPIC: DATE:

GOAL: LESSON DURATION:

LESSON OBJECTIVES

SUMMARY OF TASKS / ACTION PLAN

MATERIALS / EQUIPMENT

REFERENCES

HOME WORK / TASKS

FEEDBACK

LESSON *Planner*

SUBJECT / COURSE:

TOPIC: DATE:

GOAL: LESSON DURATION:

LESSON OBJECTIVES

SUMMARY OF TASKS / ACTION PLAN

MATERIALS / EQUIPMENT

REFERENCES

HOME WORK / TASKS

FEEDBACK

LESSON *Planner*

SUBJECT / COURSE:

TOPIC: DATE:

GOAL: LESSON DURATION:

LESSON OBJECTIVES

SUMMARY OF TASKS / ACTION PLAN

MATERIALS / EQUIPMENT

REFERENCES

HOME WORK / TASKS

FEEDBACK

LESSON *Planner*

SUBJECT / COURSE:

TOPIC:

GOAL:

DATE:

LESSON DURATION:

LESSON OBJECTIVES

SUMMARY OF TASKS / ACTION PLAN

MATERIALS / EQUIPMENT	REFERENCES

HOME WORK / TASKS	FEEDBACK

LESSON *Planner*

SUBJECT / COURSE:

TOPIC: DATE:

GOAL: LESSON DURATION:

LESSON OBJECTIVES

SUMMARY OF TASKS / ACTION PLAN

MATERIALS / EQUIPMENT

REFERENCES

HOME WORK / TASKS

FEEDBACK

LESSON *Planner*

SUBJECT / COURSE:

TOPIC: DATE:

GOAL: LESSON DURATION:

LESSON OBJECTIVES

SUMMARY OF TASKS / ACTION PLAN

MATERIALS / EQUIPMENT	REFERENCES

HOME WORK / TASKS	FEEDBACK

LESSON *Planner*

SUBJECT / COURSE:

TOPIC: **DATE:**

GOAL: **LESSON DURATION:**

LESSON OBJECTIVES

SUMMARY OF TASKS / ACTION PLAN

MATERIALS / EQUIPMENT	REFERENCES

HOME WORK / TASKS	FEEDBACK

LESSON *Planner*

SUBJECT / COURSE:

TOPIC: DATE:

GOAL: LESSON DURATION:

LESSON OBJECTIVES

SUMMARY OF TASKS / ACTION PLAN

MATERIALS / EQUIPMENT

REFERENCES

HOME WORK / TASKS

FEEDBACK

LESSON *Planner*

SUBJECT / COURSE:

TOPIC: DATE:

GOAL: LESSON DURATION:

LESSON OBJECTIVES

SUMMARY OF TASKS / ACTION PLAN

MATERIALS / EQUIPMENT

REFERENCES

HOME WORK / TASKS

FEEDBACK

LESSON *Planner*

SUBJECT / COURSE:

TOPIC: DATE:

GOAL: LESSON DURATION:

LESSON OBJECTIVES

SUMMARY OF TASKS / ACTION PLAN

MATERIALS / EQUIPMENT

REFERENCES

HOME WORK / TASKS

FEEDBACK

LESSON *Planner*

SUBJECT / COURSE:

TOPIC: DATE:

GOAL: LESSON DURATION:

LESSON OBJECTIVES

SUMMARY OF TASKS / ACTION PLAN

MATERIALS / EQUIPMENT	REFERENCES

HOME WORK / TASKS	FEEDBACK

LESSON *Planner*

SUBJECT / COURSE:

TOPIC: DATE:

GOAL: LESSON DURATION:

LESSON OBJECTIVES

SUMMARY OF TASKS / ACTION PLAN

MATERIALS / EQUIPMENT	REFERENCES

HOME WORK / TASKS	FEEDBACK

LESSON *Planner*

SUBJECT / COURSE:

TOPIC: DATE:

GOAL: LESSON DURATION:

LESSON OBJECTIVES

SUMMARY OF TASKS / ACTION PLAN

MATERIALS / EQUIPMENT

REFERENCES

HOME WORK / TASKS

FEEDBACK

LESSON *Planner*

SUBJECT / COURSE:

TOPIC: DATE:

GOAL: LESSON DURATION:

LESSON OBJECTIVES

SUMMARY OF TASKS / ACTION PLAN

MATERIALS / EQUIPMENT	REFERENCES

HOME WORK / TASKS	FEEDBACK

LESSON *Planner*

SUBJECT / COURSE:

TOPIC: DATE:

GOAL: LESSON DURATION:

LESSON OBJECTIVES

SUMMARY OF TASKS / ACTION PLAN

MATERIALS / EQUIPMENT

REFERENCES

HOME WORK / TASKS

FEEDBACK

LESSON *Planner*

SUBJECT / COURSE:

TOPIC: DATE:

GOAL: LESSON DURATION:

LESSON OBJECTIVES

SUMMARY OF TASKS / ACTION PLAN

MATERIALS / EQUIPMENT

REFERENCES

HOME WORK / TASKS

FEEDBACK

LESSON *Planner*

SUBJECT / COURSE:

TOPIC: DATE:

GOAL: LESSON DURATION:

LESSON OBJECTIVES

SUMMARY OF TASKS / ACTION PLAN

MATERIALS / EQUIPMENT

REFERENCES

HOME WORK / TASKS

FEEDBACK

LESSON *Planner*

SUBJECT / COURSE:

TOPIC: DATE:

GOAL: LESSON DURATION:

LESSON OBJECTIVES

SUMMARY OF TASKS / ACTION PLAN

MATERIALS / EQUIPMENT	REFERENCES

HOME WORK / TASKS	FEEDBACK

LESSON *Planner*

SUBJECT / COURSE:

TOPIC: DATE:

GOAL: LESSON DURATION:

LESSON OBJECTIVES

SUMMARY OF TASKS / ACTION PLAN

MATERIALS / EQUIPMENT

REFERENCES

HOME WORK / TASKS

FEEDBACK

LESSON *Planner*

SUBJECT / COURSE:

TOPIC:

DATE:

GOAL:

LESSON DURATION:

LESSON OBJECTIVES

SUMMARY OF TASKS / ACTION PLAN

MATERIALS / EQUIPMENT

REFERENCES

HOME WORK / TASKS

FEEDBACK

LESSON *Planner*

SUBJECT / COURSE:

TOPIC: DATE:

GOAL: LESSON DURATION:

LESSON OBJECTIVES

SUMMARY OF TASKS / ACTION PLAN

MATERIALS / EQUIPMENT

REFERENCES

HOME WORK / TASKS

FEEDBACK

LESSON *Planner*

SUBJECT / COURSE:

TOPIC: DATE:

GOAL: LESSON DURATION:

LESSON OBJECTIVES

SUMMARY OF TASKS / ACTION PLAN

MATERIALS / EQUIPMENT	REFERENCES

HOME WORK / TASKS	FEEDBACK

LESSON *Planner*

SUBJECT / COURSE:

TOPIC: DATE:

GOAL: LESSON DURATION:

LESSON OBJECTIVES

SUMMARY OF TASKS / ACTION PLAN

MATERIALS / EQUIPMENT

REFERENCES

HOME WORK / TASKS

FEEDBACK

LESSON *Planner*

SUBJECT / COURSE:

TOPIC: DATE:

GOAL: LESSON DURATION:

LESSON OBJECTIVES

SUMMARY OF TASKS / ACTION PLAN

MATERIALS / EQUIPMENT

REFERENCES

HOME WORK / TASKS

FEEDBACK

LESSON *Planner*

SUBJECT / COURSE:

TOPIC:

GOAL:

DATE:

LESSON DURATION:

LESSON OBJECTIVES

SUMMARY OF TASKS / ACTION PLAN

MATERIALS / EQUIPMENT

REFERENCES

HOME WORK / TASKS

FEEDBACK

LESSON *Planner*

SUBJECT / COURSE:

TOPIC: DATE:

GOAL: LESSON DURATION:

LESSON OBJECTIVES

SUMMARY OF TASKS / ACTION PLAN

MATERIALS / EQUIPMENT

REFERENCES

HOME WORK / TASKS

FEEDBACK

LESSON *Planner*

SUBJECT / COURSE:

TOPIC: DATE:

GOAL: LESSON DURATION:

LESSON OBJECTIVES

SUMMARY OF TASKS / ACTION PLAN

MATERIALS / EQUIPMENT

REFERENCES

HOME WORK / TASKS

FEEDBACK

LESSON *Planner*

SUBJECT / COURSE:

TOPIC: DATE:

GOAL: LESSON DURATION:

LESSON OBJECTIVES

SUMMARY OF TASKS / ACTION PLAN

MATERIALS / EQUIPMENT	REFERENCES

HOME WORK / TASKS	FEEDBACK

LESSON *Planner*

SUBJECT / COURSE:

TOPIC: **DATE:**

GOAL: **LESSON DURATION:**

LESSON OBJECTIVES

SUMMARY OF TASKS / ACTION PLAN

MATERIALS / EQUIPMENT

REFERENCES

HOME WORK / TASKS

FEEDBACK

LESSON *Planner*

SUBJECT / COURSE:

TOPIC: DATE:

GOAL: LESSON DURATION:

LESSON OBJECTIVES

SUMMARY OF TASKS / ACTION PLAN

MATERIALS / EQUIPMENT	REFERENCES

HOME WORK / TASKS	FEEDBACK

LESSON *Planner*

SUBJECT / COURSE:

TOPIC: **DATE:**

GOAL: **LESSON DURATION:**

LESSON OBJECTIVES

SUMMARY OF TASKS / ACTION PLAN

MATERIALS / EQUIPMENT	REFERENCES

HOME WORK / TASKS	FEEDBACK

LESSON *Planner*

SUBJECT / COURSE:

TOPIC: DATE:

GOAL: LESSON DURATION:

LESSON OBJECTIVES

SUMMARY OF TASKS / ACTION PLAN

MATERIALS / EQUIPMENT	REFERENCES

HOME WORK / TASKS	FEEDBACK

LESSON *Planner*

SUBJECT / COURSE:

TOPIC: DATE:

GOAL: LESSON DURATION:

LESSON OBJECTIVES

SUMMARY OF TASKS / ACTION PLAN

MATERIALS / EQUIPMENT

REFERENCES

HOME WORK / TASKS

FEEDBACK

LESSON *Planner*

SUBJECT / COURSE:

TOPIC:

DATE:

GOAL:

LESSON DURATION:

LESSON OBJECTIVES

SUMMARY OF TASKS / ACTION PLAN

MATERIALS / EQUIPMENT	REFERENCES

HOME WORK / TASKS	FEEDBACK

LESSON *Planner*

SUBJECT / COURSE:

TOPIC: **DATE:**

GOAL: **LESSON DURATION:**

LESSON OBJECTIVES

SUMMARY OF TASKS / ACTION PLAN

MATERIALS / EQUIPMENT

REFERENCES

HOME WORK / TASKS

FEEDBACK

LESSON *Planner*

SUBJECT / COURSE:

TOPIC: DATE:

GOAL: LESSON DURATION:

LESSON OBJECTIVES

SUMMARY OF TASKS / ACTION PLAN

MATERIALS / EQUIPMENT	REFERENCES

HOME WORK / TASKS	FEEDBACK

LESSON *Planner*

SUBJECT / COURSE:

TOPIC: DATE:

GOAL: LESSON DURATION:

LESSON OBJECTIVES

SUMMARY OF TASKS / ACTION PLAN

MATERIALS / EQUIPMENT	REFERENCES

HOME WORK / TASKS	FEEDBACK

LESSON *Planner*

SUBJECT / COURSE:

TOPIC: DATE:

GOAL: LESSON DURATION:

LESSON OBJECTIVES

SUMMARY OF TASKS / ACTION PLAN

MATERIALS / EQUIPMENT	REFERENCES

HOME WORK / TASKS	FEEDBACK

LESSON *Planner*

SUBJECT / COURSE:

TOPIC:

GOAL:

DATE:

LESSON DURATION:

LESSON OBJECTIVES

SUMMARY OF TASKS / ACTION PLAN

MATERIALS / EQUIPMENT

REFERENCES

HOME WORK / TASKS

FEEDBACK

LESSON *Planner*

SUBJECT / COURSE:

TOPIC:

GOAL:

DATE:

LESSON DURATION:

LESSON OBJECTIVES

SUMMARY OF TASKS / ACTION PLAN

MATERIALS / EQUIPMENT	REFERENCES

HOME WORK / TASKS	FEEDBACK

LESSON *Planner*

SUBJECT / COURSE:

TOPIC: DATE:

GOAL: LESSON DURATION:

LESSON OBJECTIVES

SUMMARY OF TASKS / ACTION PLAN

MATERIALS / EQUIPMENT

REFERENCES

HOME WORK / TASKS

FEEDBACK

LESSON *Planner*

SUBJECT / COURSE:

TOPIC:

DATE:

GOAL:

LESSON DURATION:

LESSON OBJECTIVES

SUMMARY OF TASKS / ACTION PLAN

MATERIALS / EQUIPMENT	REFERENCES

HOME WORK / TASKS	FEEDBACK

LESSON *Planner*

SUBJECT / COURSE:

TOPIC: DATE:

GOAL: LESSON DURATION:

LESSON OBJECTIVES

SUMMARY OF TASKS / ACTION PLAN

MATERIALS / EQUIPMENT

REFERENCES

HOME WORK / TASKS

FEEDBACK

LESSON *Planner*

SUBJECT / COURSE:

TOPIC: DATE:

GOAL: LESSON DURATION:

LESSON OBJECTIVES

SUMMARY OF TASKS / ACTION PLAN

MATERIALS / EQUIPMENT	REFERENCES

HOME WORK / TASKS	FEEDBACK

LESSON *Planner*

SUBJECT / COURSE:

TOPIC: DATE:

GOAL: LESSON DURATION:

LESSON OBJECTIVES

SUMMARY OF TASKS / ACTION PLAN

MATERIALS / EQUIPMENT

REFERENCES

HOME WORK / TASKS

FEEDBACK

LESSON *Planner*

SUBJECT / COURSE:

TOPIC: DATE:

GOAL: LESSON DURATION:

LESSON OBJECTIVES

SUMMARY OF TASKS / ACTION PLAN

MATERIALS / EQUIPMENT	REFERENCES

HOME WORK / TASKS	FEEDBACK

LESSON *Planner*

SUBJECT / COURSE:

TOPIC: DATE:

GOAL: LESSON DURATION:

LESSON OBJECTIVES

SUMMARY OF TASKS / ACTION PLAN

MATERIALS / EQUIPMENT

REFERENCES

HOME WORK / TASKS

FEEDBACK

LESSON *Planner*

SUBJECT / COURSE:

TOPIC: DATE:

GOAL: LESSON DURATION:

LESSON OBJECTIVES

SUMMARY OF TASKS / ACTION PLAN

MATERIALS / EQUIPMENT	REFERENCES

HOME WORK / TASKS	FEEDBACK

LESSON *Planner*

SUBJECT / COURSE:

TOPIC: DATE:

GOAL: LESSON DURATION:

LESSON OBJECTIVES

SUMMARY OF TASKS / ACTION PLAN

MATERIALS / EQUIPMENT

REFERENCES

HOME WORK / TASKS

FEEDBACK

LESSON *Planner*

SUBJECT / COURSE:

TOPIC: DATE:

GOAL: LESSON DURATION:

LESSON OBJECTIVES

SUMMARY OF TASKS / ACTION PLAN

MATERIALS / EQUIPMENT

REFERENCES

HOME WORK / TASKS

FEEDBACK

LESSON *Planner*

SUBJECT / COURSE:

TOPIC: DATE:

GOAL: LESSON DURATION:

LESSON OBJECTIVES

SUMMARY OF TASKS / ACTION PLAN

MATERIALS / EQUIPMENT	REFERENCES

HOME WORK / TASKS	FEEDBACK

LESSON *Planner*

SUBJECT / COURSE:

TOPIC: DATE:

GOAL: LESSON DURATION:

LESSON OBJECTIVES

SUMMARY OF TASKS / ACTION PLAN

MATERIALS / EQUIPMENT

REFERENCES

HOME WORK / TASKS

FEEDBACK

LESSON *Planner*

SUBJECT / COURSE:

TOPIC: DATE:

GOAL: LESSON DURATION:

LESSON OBJECTIVES

SUMMARY OF TASKS / ACTION PLAN

MATERIALS / EQUIPMENT

REFERENCES

HOME WORK / TASKS

FEEDBACK

LESSON *Planner*

SUBJECT / COURSE:

TOPIC: DATE:

GOAL: LESSON DURATION:

LESSON OBJECTIVES

SUMMARY OF TASKS / ACTION PLAN

MATERIALS / EQUIPMENT

REFERENCES

HOME WORK / TASKS

FEEDBACK

LESSON *Planner*

SUBJECT / COURSE:

TOPIC: DATE:

GOAL: LESSON DURATION:

LESSON OBJECTIVES

SUMMARY OF TASKS / ACTION PLAN

MATERIALS / EQUIPMENT	REFERENCES

HOME WORK / TASKS	FEEDBACK

LESSON *Planner*

SUBJECT / COURSE:

TOPIC: DATE:

GOAL: LESSON DURATION:

LESSON OBJECTIVES

SUMMARY OF TASKS / ACTION PLAN

MATERIALS / EQUIPMENT	REFERENCES

HOME WORK / TASKS	FEEDBACK

LESSON *Planner*

SUBJECT / COURSE:

TOPIC:

GOAL:

DATE:

LESSON DURATION:

LESSON OBJECTIVES

SUMMARY OF TASKS / ACTION PLAN

MATERIALS / EQUIPMENT	REFERENCES

HOME WORK / TASKS	FEEDBACK

LESSON *Planner*

SUBJECT / COURSE:

TOPIC: DATE:

GOAL: LESSON DURATION:

LESSON OBJECTIVES

SUMMARY OF TASKS / ACTION PLAN

MATERIALS / EQUIPMENT	REFERENCES

HOME WORK / TASKS	FEEDBACK

LESSON *Planner*

SUBJECT / COURSE:

TOPIC: DATE:

GOAL: LESSON DURATION:

LESSON OBJECTIVES

SUMMARY OF TASKS / ACTION PLAN

MATERIALS / EQUIPMENT	REFERENCES

HOME WORK / TASKS	FEEDBACK

LESSON *Planner*

SUBJECT / COURSE:

TOPIC:

DATE:

GOAL:

LESSON DURATION:

LESSON OBJECTIVES

SUMMARY OF TASKS / ACTION PLAN

MATERIALS / EQUIPMENT

REFERENCES

HOME WORK / TASKS

FEEDBACK

LESSON *Planner*

SUBJECT / COURSE:

TOPIC: DATE:

GOAL: LESSON DURATION:

LESSON OBJECTIVES

SUMMARY OF TASKS / ACTION PLAN

MATERIALS / EQUIPMENT

REFERENCES

HOME WORK / TASKS

FEEDBACK

LESSON *Planner*

SUBJECT / COURSE:

TOPIC: DATE:

GOAL: LESSON DURATION:

LESSON OBJECTIVES

SUMMARY OF TASKS / ACTION PLAN

MATERIALS / EQUIPMENT	REFERENCES

HOME WORK / TASKS	FEEDBACK

LESSON *Planner*

SUBJECT / COURSE:

TOPIC: DATE:

GOAL: LESSON DURATION:

LESSON OBJECTIVES

SUMMARY OF TASKS / ACTION PLAN

MATERIALS / EQUIPMENT

REFERENCES

HOME WORK / TASKS

FEEDBACK

LESSON *Planner*

SUBJECT / COURSE:

TOPIC:

GOAL:

DATE:

LESSON DURATION:

LESSON OBJECTIVES

SUMMARY OF TASKS / ACTION PLAN

MATERIALS / EQUIPMENT

REFERENCES

HOME WORK / TASKS

FEEDBACK

LESSON *Planner*

SUBJECT / COURSE:

TOPIC: DATE:

GOAL: LESSON DURATION:

LESSON OBJECTIVES

SUMMARY OF TASKS / ACTION PLAN

MATERIALS / EQUIPMENT

REFERENCES

HOME WORK / TASKS

FEEDBACK

LESSON *Planner*

SUBJECT / COURSE:

TOPIC: DATE:

GOAL: LESSON DURATION:

LESSON OBJECTIVES

SUMMARY OF TASKS / ACTION PLAN

MATERIALS / EQUIPMENT

REFERENCES

HOME WORK / TASKS

FEEDBACK

LESSON *Planner*

SUBJECT / COURSE:

TOPIC: DATE:

GOAL: LESSON DURATION:

LESSON OBJECTIVES

SUMMARY OF TASKS / ACTION PLAN

MATERIALS / EQUIPMENT

REFERENCES

HOME WORK / TASKS

FEEDBACK

LESSON *Planner*

SUBJECT / COURSE:

TOPIC: DATE:

GOAL: LESSON DURATION:

LESSON OBJECTIVES

SUMMARY OF TASKS / ACTION PLAN

MATERIALS / EQUIPMENT

REFERENCES

HOME WORK / TASKS

FEEDBACK

LESSON *Planner*

SUBJECT / COURSE:

TOPIC: DATE:

GOAL: LESSON DURATION:

LESSON OBJECTIVES

SUMMARY OF TASKS / ACTION PLAN

MATERIALS / EQUIPMENT

REFERENCES

HOME WORK / TASKS

FEEDBACK

LESSON *Planner*

SUBJECT / COURSE:

TOPIC: DATE:

GOAL: LESSON DURATION:

LESSON OBJECTIVES

SUMMARY OF TASKS / ACTION PLAN

MATERIALS / EQUIPMENT

REFERENCES

HOME WORK / TASKS

FEEDBACK

LESSON *Planner*

SUBJECT / COURSE:

TOPIC:

GOAL:

DATE:

LESSON DURATION:

LESSON OBJECTIVES

SUMMARY OF TASKS / ACTION PLAN

MATERIALS / EQUIPMENT	REFERENCES

HOME WORK / TASKS	FEEDBACK

LESSON *Planner*

SUBJECT / COURSE:

TOPIC: DATE:

GOAL: LESSON DURATION:

LESSON OBJECTIVES

SUMMARY OF TASKS / ACTION PLAN

MATERIALS / EQUIPMENT

REFERENCES

HOME WORK / TASKS

FEEDBACK

LESSON *Planner*

SUBJECT / COURSE:

TOPIC: DATE:

GOAL: LESSON DURATION:

LESSON OBJECTIVES

SUMMARY OF TASKS / ACTION PLAN

MATERIALS / EQUIPMENT

REFERENCES

HOME WORK / TASKS

FEEDBACK

LESSON *Planner*

SUBJECT / COURSE:

TOPIC: DATE:

GOAL: LESSON DURATION:

LESSON OBJECTIVES

SUMMARY OF TASKS / ACTION PLAN

MATERIALS / EQUIPMENT	REFERENCES

HOME WORK / TASKS	FEEDBACK

LESSON *Planner*

SUBJECT / COURSE:

TOPIC: DATE:

GOAL: LESSON DURATION:

LESSON OBJECTIVES

SUMMARY OF TASKS / ACTION PLAN

MATERIALS / EQUIPMENT

REFERENCES

HOME WORK / TASKS

FEEDBACK

LESSON *Planner*

SUBJECT / COURSE:

TOPIC:

GOAL:

DATE:

LESSON DURATION:

LESSON OBJECTIVES

SUMMARY OF TASKS / ACTION PLAN

MATERIALS / EQUIPMENT	REFERENCES

HOME WORK / TASKS	FEEDBACK

LESSON *Planner*

SUBJECT / COURSE:

TOPIC: DATE:

GOAL: LESSON DURATION:

LESSON OBJECTIVES

SUMMARY OF TASKS / ACTION PLAN

MATERIALS / EQUIPMENT

REFERENCES

HOME WORK / TASKS

FEEDBACK

LESSON *Planner*

SUBJECT / COURSE:

TOPIC: DATE:

GOAL: LESSON DURATION:

LESSON OBJECTIVES

SUMMARY OF TASKS / ACTION PLAN

MATERIALS / EQUIPMENT	REFERENCES

HOME WORK / TASKS	FEEDBACK

LESSON *Planner*

SUBJECT / COURSE:

TOPIC: DATE:

GOAL: LESSON DURATION:

LESSON OBJECTIVES

SUMMARY OF TASKS / ACTION PLAN

MATERIALS / EQUIPMENT	REFERENCES

HOME WORK / TASKS	FEEDBACK

LESSON *Planner*

SUBJECT / COURSE:

TOPIC: DATE:

GOAL: LESSON DURATION:

LESSON OBJECTIVES

SUMMARY OF TASKS / ACTION PLAN

MATERIALS / EQUIPMENT

REFERENCES

HOME WORK / TASKS

FEEDBACK

LESSON *Planner*

SUBJECT / COURSE:

TOPIC:

DATE:

GOAL:

LESSON DURATION:

LESSON OBJECTIVES

SUMMARY OF TASKS / ACTION PLAN

MATERIALS / EQUIPMENT

REFERENCES

HOME WORK / TASKS

FEEDBACK

LESSON *Planner*

SUBJECT / COURSE:

TOPIC: DATE:

GOAL: LESSON DURATION:

LESSON OBJECTIVES

SUMMARY OF TASKS / ACTION PLAN

MATERIALS / EQUIPMENT

REFERENCES

HOME WORK / TASKS

FEEDBACK

LESSON *Planner*

SUBJECT / COURSE:

TOPIC: DATE:

GOAL: LESSON DURATION:

LESSON OBJECTIVES

SUMMARY OF TASKS / ACTION PLAN

MATERIALS / EQUIPMENT

REFERENCES

HOME WORK / TASKS

FEEDBACK

LESSON *Planner*

SUBJECT / COURSE:

TOPIC: DATE:

GOAL: LESSON DURATION:

LESSON OBJECTIVES

SUMMARY OF TASKS / ACTION PLAN

MATERIALS / EQUIPMENT

REFERENCES

HOME WORK / TASKS

FEEDBACK

LESSON *Planner*

SUBJECT / COURSE:

TOPIC: DATE:

GOAL: LESSON DURATION:

LESSON OBJECTIVES

SUMMARY OF TASKS / ACTION PLAN

MATERIALS / EQUIPMENT	REFERENCES

HOME WORK / TASKS	FEEDBACK

LESSON *Planner*

SUBJECT / COURSE:

TOPIC: DATE:

GOAL: LESSON DURATION:

LESSON OBJECTIVES

SUMMARY OF TASKS / ACTION PLAN

MATERIALS / EQUIPMENT	REFERENCES

HOME WORK / TASKS	FEEDBACK

LESSON *Planner*

SUBJECT / COURSE:

TOPIC: DATE:

GOAL: LESSON DURATION:

LESSON OBJECTIVES

SUMMARY OF TASKS / ACTION PLAN

MATERIALS / EQUIPMENT

REFERENCES

HOME WORK / TASKS

FEEDBACK

LESSON *Planner*

SUBJECT / COURSE:

TOPIC: DATE:

GOAL: LESSON DURATION:

LESSON OBJECTIVES

SUMMARY OF TASKS / ACTION PLAN

MATERIALS / EQUIPMENT

REFERENCES

HOME WORK / TASKS

FEEDBACK

LESSON *Planner*

SUBJECT / COURSE:

TOPIC: DATE:

GOAL: LESSON DURATION:

LESSON OBJECTIVES

SUMMARY OF TASKS / ACTION PLAN

MATERIALS / EQUIPMENT

REFERENCES

HOME WORK / TASKS

FEEDBACK

LESSON *Planner*

SUBJECT / COURSE:

TOPIC: DATE:

GOAL: LESSON DURATION:

LESSON OBJECTIVES

SUMMARY OF TASKS / ACTION PLAN

MATERIALS / EQUIPMENT

REFERENCES

HOME WORK / TASKS

FEEDBACK

LESSON *Planner*

SUBJECT / COURSE:

TOPIC: DATE:

GOAL: LESSON DURATION:

LESSON OBJECTIVES

SUMMARY OF TASKS / ACTION PLAN

MATERIALS / EQUIPMENT	REFERENCES

HOME WORK / TASKS	FEEDBACK

LESSON *Planner*

SUBJECT / COURSE:

TOPIC: DATE:

GOAL: LESSON DURATION:

LESSON OBJECTIVES

SUMMARY OF TASKS / ACTION PLAN

MATERIALS / EQUIPMENT

REFERENCES

HOME WORK / TASKS

FEEDBACK

LESSON *Planner*

SUBJECT / COURSE:

TOPIC: DATE:

GOAL: LESSON DURATION:

LESSON OBJECTIVES

SUMMARY OF TASKS / ACTION PLAN

MATERIALS / EQUIPMENT

REFERENCES

HOME WORK / TASKS

FEEDBACK

LESSON *Planner*

SUBJECT / COURSE:

TOPIC: DATE:

GOAL: LESSON DURATION:

LESSON OBJECTIVES

SUMMARY OF TASKS / ACTION PLAN

MATERIALS / EQUIPMENT

REFERENCES

HOME WORK / TASKS

FEEDBACK

LESSON *Planner*

SUBJECT / COURSE:

TOPIC: DATE:

GOAL: LESSON DURATION:

LESSON OBJECTIVES

SUMMARY OF TASKS / ACTION PLAN

MATERIALS / EQUIPMENT	REFERENCES

HOME WORK / TASKS	FEEDBACK

LESSON *Planner*

SUBJECT / COURSE:

TOPIC: DATE:

GOAL: LESSON DURATION:

LESSON OBJECTIVES

SUMMARY OF TASKS / ACTION PLAN

MATERIALS / EQUIPMENT

REFERENCES

HOME WORK / TASKS

FEEDBACK

LESSON *Planner*

SUBJECT / COURSE:

TOPIC: DATE:

GOAL: LESSON DURATION:

LESSON OBJECTIVES

SUMMARY OF TASKS / ACTION PLAN

MATERIALS / EQUIPMENT

REFERENCES

HOME WORK / TASKS

FEEDBACK

CPSIA information can be obtained
at www.ICGtesting.com
Printed in the USA
BVHW090035260221
601128BV00010B/987